BEST MADEIRA CAKE RECIPE

How to make the best tasty and mouthwatering Madeira cake.

Copyright@2023

Udenta Mercy

1

Chapter One

BEST MADEIRA CAKE RECIPE

Searching for a mouthwatering and flexible sponge recipe? This Madeira cake recipe is the best one for you. The best kind of sponge for layered cakes, as the sponge is sufficiently able to keep the cake strong when stacked

The best Madeira cake recipe that is simple, heavenly and trusted! This customary Madeira cake is light, delicate, and damp with a firm surface. Ideal for regular baking or cut and designed for events.

Madeira cake and sponge cakes are two of my most heated cakes! As a past part-time expert cake producer, I have prepared many cakes in the course of my life and I can say I have excelled at cake baking. Truth be told my cake baking days began when I was a

young lady when I would help my mum make cakes available to be purchased at the general store she claimed then. Bygone times. I actually prepare cakes for my family or more all, I appreciate eating cakes.

Cakes unite individuals, whether for evening tea, festivity, treat at home or gatherings, youngsters

and grown-ups like to have a cut
or more. This cake recipe is
perhaps of the most
straightforward cake you'll heat.

MADEIRA CAKE RECIPE

Madeira cake is a kind of English sponge cake that got its name from Madeira wine, a Portuguese wine that was well known in Britain during the 1800s. Customary Madeira cake isn't made of wine yet was famously presented with Madeira wine in those days during the 1800s thus its name. Madeira cake can be presented with teas and utilized in festival cakes.

This is the best Madeira cake recipe and anybody can make it. At the point when next you go shopping for food before you connect for that store Madeira cake, recollect you can make yours in simple tasks, you'll know precisely exact thing's in your hand crafted cake, no secret additives and you can make as much cake as you need at whatever point you need.

Here, I have included devices you'll require, fixings, estimations, how to make Madeira cake, tips, how to store from there, the sky is the limit. Allow me to tell you the best way to simplify Madeira cake in simple tasks.

Chapter Two

DIFFERENCE BETWEEN MADEIRA CAKE AND VICTORIA CAKE

No, it's not. Despite the fact that Madeira cake is a kind of sponge cake and uses the equivalent creaming strategy as pound cake and victoria sponge cake, it has a denser surface than victoria sponge cake. Madeira cake is made with more flour than victoria sponge and has a firmer surface and is, thusly, more reasonable for cutting as it holds shape when cut and chilled. It's great for festivity cakes like wedding cakes. Madeira cake arches and break at the top during baking.

Tools FOR BAKING CAKE

To make this recipe and for most cake recipes, you'll require these straightforward instruments:

Blending bowl - A blending bowl sufficiently large to contain the cake hitter and leave space for blending.

Mixer - Hand or stand mixer. I for the most part utilize a hand mixer for my cakes as they are more helpful for me.

Spatula - To scratch the sides of the blending bowl and crease the flour in.

Cake Dish - Portion tin for Madeira portion cake, round cake search for gold 8 and 10".

Baking paper - Additionally called material paper. This is to line the cake dish so the cake emerges from the container neatly in the wake of baking.

Cake analyzer - Stick or toothpick will in all actuality do fine. This is to test cake doneness.

Cooling rack - To cool cakes on.

Chapter Three

INGRIDIENTS FOR MADEIRA CAKE

You really want only a few of ingredients for this cake recipe (Definite fixing rundown and bearing in the recipe card at the lower part of this page) and they are:

Margarine - Bring to room temperature.

Sugar-Granulated or Caster sugar

Eggs - Bring to room temperature

Milk

Self-raising flour - Filtered. In the event that you don't have self-raising flour, you can make it by adding a teaspoon of baking powder to each 200g of plain flour.

Lemon or Orange enhancing or Vanilla concentrate - Utilize one of these seasoning.

Lemon or orange zing - For lemon

Madeira cake or orange Madeira cake

Chapter Four

STEP BY STEP INSTRUCTION TO MAKE MADEIRA CAKE

Ensure your fixings are all at room temperature.

Focus on margarine the cake container and line with baking paper/material paper. Put dish away.

In a blending bowl, include spread and sugar then utilize a mixer to blend till player is light and fleecy.

Break eggs in a separate bowl (I like to do this so on the off chance that there's any rotten one in the bunch, you could not have possibly destroyed your player). Add lemon or orange or vanilla seasoning to the eggs and whisk.

Pour the whisked eggs in the spread and sugar blend and blend in with the mixer for a couple of moments.

Add flour in the player and blend in with a spatula. Overlap in till combined.

flour included the player and collapsed in.

Pour cake player in lined cake dish and spot in preheated stove. Heat at temperature of 170C for

45 minutes or till a cake analyzer tells the truth.

Madeira cake hitter poured in cake skillet

Turn cake onto a cooling rack and pass on to cool.

Straight from the broiler Madeira cake

LEMON MADEIRA CAKE RECIPE

For lemon Madeira cake, utilize the fixings and headings here yet where the fixing list showed seasoning, use lemon enhancing (lemon concentrate) and zing of an entire lemon.

IS MADEIRA CAKE A POUND CAKE

No, it's not. They are comparable anyway pound cake is made with pound estimations for every one of the fixings.

Ways to make MADEIRA CAKE

Make sure to preheat stove at temperature prior to putting cake hitter in the broiler. If utilizing a traditional stove, preheat at a temperature of 170C/gas mark 3 and for fan broiler it's 150-160C.

Put cake skillet and prepare cake in the broiler for best intensity circulation.

Overlap the flour in with a spatula (as suggested in the headings) as opposed to utilizing hand mixer.

Don't over mix player once the flour has gone in or you could wind up with thick cake.

Put the player in the broiler right away.

You can add any kind of enhancing like orange, lemon, nutmeg.

Try not to open the stove in the initial 20 minutes while the cake is baking. This could make the cake sink in the center. You can open towards the finish of baking opportunity to check for doneness.

Cool cake on a cooling rack.

Look at these other astonishing cake recipes simple coconut cake recipe, basic banana cake and carrot cake.

The most effective method to STORE

Madeira cake tastes better the following day. Cakes can remain securely at room temperature for as long as 5 days, notwithstanding, it's ideal to refrigerate. Permit cake to cool totally and wrap firmly in clingfilm or foil, put in cooler packs and store in the refrigerator for as long as 5 days or in the cooler for up a half year.

Best Madeira Cake Recipe

The best Madeira cake recipe that is simple, heavenly and trusted! This customary Madeira cake is light, delicate, and soggy with a firm surface. Ideal for regular baking or cut and designed for events.

Planning Time

15 minutes

Cook Time

45 minutes

All out Time

1 hour

Hardware:

Broiler

Cake skillet/Portion tin

Fixings:

150 g Margarine

150 g Sugar

3 little Eggs

150 g Self raising flour

50 g Plain flour

1 tablespoon Milk

1 teaspoon Enhancing orange or lemon or vanilla

1 Zing of entire Orange or Lemon (for orange or lemon Madeira cake)

For 8" round Madeira cake, twofold this recipe and offer cake player in two 8 inch cake dish.

Guidelines

Ensure your fixings are all at room temperature.

Focus on margarine the cake skillet and line with baking paper/material paper. Put dish away.

In a blending bowl, include spread and sugar then, at that point, use mixer to blend till player is light and soft. Break eggs in a separate bowl (I like to do this so in case there's any rotten one in the bunch, you could not have possibly demolished your hitter).

Add milk, lemon or orange or vanilla enhancing to the eggs and whisk. Add the whisked eggs in the margarine and sugar blend and blend in with the mixer for few moments.

Add flour in the hitter and blend in with spatula. Crease in till consolidated.

Pour cake hitter in lined cake container and spot in pre warmed stove. Heat at temperature of 170C for 45 minutes or till cake analyzer tells the truth.

Turn cake onto cooling rack and pass on to cool.

Cut cake and appreciate.

LEMON MADEIRA CAKE RECIPE

For lemon Madeira cake, utilize the fixings and bearings here however where the fixing list showed enhancing, use lemon seasoning (lemon concentrate) and zing of entire lemon.

*For 8" round Madeira cake, twofold this recipe and offer cake player in two 8 inch cake dish.

Tips

Make sure to preheat the stove prior to putting the cake hitter in the broiler. If utilizing a traditional broiler, preheat at a temperature of 170C/gas mark 3 and for fan stove is 150-160C.

Put cake skillet and prepare the cake in the stove for best intensity circulation.

Crease the flour in with a spatula (as suggested in the headings) as opposed to utilizing a hand mixer.

Don't over mix player once the flour has gone in or you could wind up with thick cake.

Put the player in the stove right away.

You can add any kind of flavor

Chapter Five

THE ORIGIN OF MADEIRA CAKE

Madeira cake is a rich cake item falling under the class of sponge cake. This commonly shows that the cake is utilized shortening. The cake began in Britain around the 1800s.

However the name has persuaded some to think that this cake has beginnings in the Portuguese islands, it is really named for the wine it frequently goes with. Madeira wine, created on the Madeira Islands, was a well-known drink in Europe as soon as the sixteenth hundred years. The ocean journey from the Madeira Islands to Europe, and later to America, helped age the wine. The intensity of the boat and steady development on the ocean were useful to the completed item.

Madeira cake was created as a backup to this most loved cocktail. This sort of cake is thick, soggy, and wealthy in flavor. The principal fixings are exceptionally straightforward, generally comprising just of margarine, sugar, eggs, and flour.

Lemon curd, which is some of the time used to top Madeira cake.

Traditional versions of this cake are given a lemon flavoring. Lemon juice and lemon rind are added to the recipe to provide it with a slightly tangy taste. Modern variations on the recipe, however, may deviate from this. Lime juice and lime rind can be substituted to create a lime variety of Madeira cake. Another popular variation that is often served today is vanilla Madeira cake, made by replacing the lemon juice and zest with vanilla extract.

☐

Caution

Do not open the oven in the first 20 minutes while the cake is baking. This might cause the cake to sink in the middle. You can open towards the end of baking time to check for doneness

Nutrition:

Calories: 321kcal | Carbohydrates: 37g | Protein: 5g | Fat: 17g | Saturated Fat: 10g | Cholesterol: 100mg | Sodium: 158mg | Potassium: 52mg | Fiber: 1g | Sugar: 19g | Vitamin A: 555IU | Calcium: 18mg | Iron: 1mg

Printed in Great Britain
by Amazon

37879866R00020